The Story of Lord Jagannatha

Retold and Illustrated by
R. Guru

All rights reserved.
© R.Guru 2017
No part of this publication maybe reproduced without permission.
rguruwrites@gmail.com

Dedication

Dedicated to my spiritual master and eternal father
His Divine Grace
A.C. Bhaktivedanta Swami Prabhupada

King Indradyumna's greatest wish was to see God. He inquired from many saints where he could see Him.

One day a pilgrim passing his kingdom described the beauty of God in the form of Nilamadhava residing in Utkala desa in the east coast of India. King Indradyumna was thrilled. He sent his royal priest Vidyapati to locate the exact place.

After searching for months Vidyapati came to a beautiful village.

He was tired and fell ill during his stay in the village. Visvavasu, the leader of the Sabara tribe and his beautiful daughter Lalita took good care of him.

He, then married Lalita according to her father's wish.

During his stay, Vidyapati noticed that Visvavasu left home every morning. He returned looking radiant wearing sweet smelling sandalwood tilak and flower garland made up of exotic forest flowers.

"Where does your father go? My dear wife, please tell me," Vidyapati asked his wife Lalita. She hesitated to reveal her father's secret. But he insisted.

"Well, my father goes to worship Sri Nilamadhava in the forest. I know you are here for Him. I will request my father to take you along with him," she said.

Visvavasu, however, refused to take Vidyapati, for he feared the Lord may disappear if he revealed His place.

He finally agreed upon one condition. He would take him blind folded.

The next day Visvavasu took Vidyapati blind-folded on a bullock cart and guided him to the top of Nilachala hill, the eternal abode of Sri Nilamadhava.

Clever Vidyapati dropped mustard seeds all along the path, hoping the seeds would grow into plants bearing bright yellow flowers in the next rain.

Upon reaching the spot, Visvavasu opened Vidyāpati's blindfold. Lord Nilamadhava was most beautiful with four hands decorated with His divine disc, conch, club and lotus flower.

While Vidyapati adored the Lord, Visvavasu went further into the forest to collect wild flowers and fruits for worship. Just then Vidyapati witnessed something wonderful.

A sleepy crow that perched on a tree fell into a pond below. Rising from the water, the crow transformed into a beautiful God-like form and rose towards the sky.

Vidyapati was wonder-struck. He wanted to jump into the pond following the crow.

At that time, Sri Nilamadhava spoke in a sweet voice. "My dear Vidyapati, your duty is to inform King Indradyumna about my location. Go and tell him without fail."

After days of travel, the king and his retinue reached Nilachala hill guided by the mustard flowers.

But, by the time they reached Nilachala hill, Sri Nilamadhava had disappeared.

King Indradyumna was greatly disappointed and felt unfortunate that he couldn't see the Lord.

In a short while, a divine voice was heard from the sky.

"King Indradyumna, do not be sad. You can see me in a special dharu brahman wooden form as Jagannatha along with my elder brother Baladeva and sister Subhadra. Go to the sea shore and find three blocks of wood drifting towards you. Carve my form from it and worship me with grandeur for the benefit of all."

The jubilant king reached the shore and received the special wood. He invited Visvavasu to handle the passage of dharu brahman to the palace where they would be carved into deities.

At the palace the king faced another hurdle. No sculptor was able to lay his chisel on the wood. The sharp tools broke into pieces.

Vishwakarma, the architect of the heavens came disguised as an old man. He promised to complete the carving within twenty-one days behind closed doors. No one should disturb him.

After two weeks of carving, the king became anxious because he could not hear any chiselling sound from inside.

Fearing the old man may have died and also upon the insistence of his queen Gundicha, he opened the doors before time.

The deities of Lord Jagannatha, Baladeva and Subhadra were half carved. They had no legs and had incomplete hands. There was no sign of the old sculptor. King Indradyumna was devastated. He sat on a fast giving up food and water, punishing himself for his hastiness which rendered the deities half-finished.

Sri Jagannatha Temple
Puri

The same voice sounded again to pacify the king.

"Dear king, do not be harsh on yourself. This is my special form that I took long ago when I experienced the love of my dear most devotees, the gopies of Vrindavana. It is my desire that this form be seen by all my devotees. You have played your part in making this happen."

King Indradyumna regained his will to live. He built a magnificent temple in Puri. Lord Brahma installed the divine weapon, Sudharshana chakra on the temple tower.

Sri Jagannatha

Subhadra Devi

Sri Baladeva

Anyone who visits Jagannatha Puri and worships the beautiful forms of Sri Jagannatha, Baladeva and Subhadra Devi is never born again in this material world.

He gets freedom from repeated birth, death, old-age and disease.

Jai Jagannatha! Jai Baladeva! Jai Subhadra!

Colour your own Lord Jagannatha.

You can tell this small prayer to Lord Jagannatha everyday:

> Jagannatha swami
> nayana-patha-gami
> bhavatu me
>
> May that Jagannatha Swami be the object of my vision.

Hare Krishna Hare Krishna
Krishna Krishna Hare Hare
Hare Rama Hare Rama
Rama Rama Hare Hare